A touch, a tear, a tempest

Sanober Khan

Copyright© 2012 Sanober Khan

ISBN 978-81-8253-206-9

First Edition: 2012

₹ 200/-

Cyberwit.net

HIG 45 Kaushambi Kunj, Kalindipuram

Allahabad - 211011 (U.P.) India

http://www.cyberwit.net

Tel: +(91) 9415091004 +(91) (532) 2552257
E-mail: info@cyberwit.net

Printed at Repro India Limited.

To my Mom and Dad,
for all the beauty and joy you have
brought me
I will always be your little dove

Contents

Poetic Toast

To mornings,
That deserve the melodic kiss
Of songbirds

To the oceans,
That deserve the balletic dance
of the sun

To people,
who deserve warm,
mama-bear hugs,

To the labourers,
Who deserve ice-tea breaks
And a permanent house to come home to

To breezy days,
That deserve the union
of two old friends,

To the rain,
That deserves the joyous arms
of a child,
& romantic sips of cappuccino

To the newborns,
That deserve a lifetime
Of being wrapped in love,
Safety and sanctity

To the newlyweds,
That deserve every blessing
To have ever escaped the heavens

To the wounded,
who deserve a soft,
Healing, human touch

To Sundays,
That deserve lazy stretches,
And hammock dreams,

To summers,
That deserve delicious naps,
And laughter-filled barbecues

To mothers,
Who deserve to be rewarded
Beyond gratitude-filled kisses,
And prayers,

To the poets,
Who deserve the admiration
Of every heart

To the human body,
That deserves the pleasure of workouts,
Yoga, and healthy meals,

To the forgivers, and the forgiven,
Who deserve a peaceful night's sleep

To the street urchins,
Who deserve the love of family,
And a beautiful home

To starry nights,
That deserve the passion of lovers,
& the whispers of soft melted souls,

To moments,
That deserve...
profound poems

And to memories,
that deserve...
wistful tears.

Touched My heart

When you touched my heart,
oh friend, I realized,
flowers were never merely
a fragrance,

the morning skies had never been
just a unicorn....of silver
peach, and blue

Coffee was not merely
...just a good listener

butterflies were never just
blown kisses...in the wind

words were always more
than just silk...against the soul

I realized,
I was more than
just a sentient being
filled with tender aches
with feelings running
out of the nectar of spirit

with eyes more than just a nest
for the birds,

I realized,
June had never been...just a month
music....never just a tremble
on my lips

warmth was never
merely a blanket

and love was never meant to be..
just a metaphor
between the pages of poetry

You touched my heart...ever so softly
and I realized,
tears had never been....merely salt

and the Rain...oh the Rain!
had never been merely water

Kisses

Kisses don't always mean
the melting melody
of meeting lips

or the warm swirling
of pecks on cheeks

or..
the silken union
Of skin and skin

But kisses happen
When my eyes alight
on the feathers
of the cotton-white songbird

when my morning
blueberry muffin
sails slowly
upon my savouring tongue

when my freshly shampooed hair
catch the stray shafts of sunlight
in one sweeping motion

when my hands skim along
the furs
of a meadow rabbit

kisses bubble...
when the rain
hits the asphalt in my soul
giving rise to fragrant verses

when the ocean mist
engulfs me, like a lifetime's
friendship honoured

when a winter jacket
is lovingly wrapped
round my fragile shoulders

when I gently lay a blanket
on my sleeping mother

when the frogs of laughter
go splashing
in a pond of tears

kisses explode

when...

someone
believes in me

when my heart cries out
a song of thanks
to yours

when my lashes
fold together, each night

laden heavily
with prayer

when love
wounds me
with soft pillows
with tender lips and fingers

And when...

I realize
that kisses... are, and always will be
the only language
that I will have ever truly known.

I Can Hear

Spring has begun to chirp already
its melody, opening before me
like a creamy cocoon

the streets have begun to tune
into the bustle...of cafés and cars
high-fives and celebration

laughter has already arrived
it seems, on its carriage
of happy faces,

even the blush has started to return
to the apple blossom's cheeks

i can already hear, the noon time's
lullabies to peace, the evening's
tear-wiped waltz ...to jubilation

i can already feel, the night's music,
from its pulsing dance floors,
to its moon singing
to every ounce of her last breath

even sorrows of the broken spirited,
seem to be tapping
to rhythm of the melting stream

it's that lovely morning again,
with the same sun-glossed lips,
ready to be kissed again

the same world washing itself
of elegies, with birds and blooms
sighs and songs,

ready to embrace,
another glorious day,
it's all beautiful....really,
and yet so cruel

the sound of your silence
against the sound

of life going on...

I Wouldn't Mind

I wouldn't mind...
if life left me...

wingless

burnt to cinders,
ripped by storms,
scattered...like weeds

celestially wounded

without cherry blossoms
to perish with

but I would cry
with head held in my hands
if it left me...

unfulfilled.

Some Cold Morning

Someday,
Some cold morning...
I know, I will awaken
To a world very different, from mine,
.....Very distant

When I peel,
My eyes open,
A lot of things, will have changed,
The curtains frayed...
The trees barren...
Someone,
A thousand skies away...

The birds will be singing to a different tune
The lines in my palms will have a deeper hue

Millions and millions....
Of years, will have passed
And yet...it will feel like
We'd only just...brushed past

And so many colours
I will have seen...
The menacing greys,
And pine greens
The soft pink and purples,
Of spring,

And summer blue
And so many others
Without you

And I will have lost...something precious,
Because of the choice I made today,
So many times I will have been broken,
Rebuilt, and replaced

So much pain,
I will have tried..
To overcome,
A friend's betrayal
and the loss... of a loved one
So many rejections,
I will have faced,
All the while struggling
To be someone...

And so many seasons,
Shall come and go,
So many faces
I will never know,
While my desires...
Will have spun a web
Of unseen glory
Along with my wrinkled skin...
Telling its own story...

And I know someday...
I shall awaken
To a morning of a world I made,
Out of my own thoughts,
My own sweat....and my own mistakes

And as my tears start to fall
with promises ....I no longer can keep
You and I, We'll both know,
It is time for me to
.....Go back to sleep.

Predicament

sometimes I am not sure
when I love the sky more

when it's soaked in the melting,
golden soufflé of the sun

or when its hooded, with silver eyes,
brooding, in liquid melancholy

i am not sure sometimes
what makes me happier

watching the morning glimmer
through the gauzy wings
of a dragonfly

or having a giant butterfly
crash against me

having a gallon of cookies & cream
from Häagen-Dazs, all to myself
or devouring cotton candy,
and ice lollies by the beach

reading a heart caressing book
in a couch of stars
or moments spent with a friend
in comfortable silence

i can't always tell what's better
the scent of daffodils
or baby powder

long drives
in the star-spangled deserts
or long walks
along winding tea gardens

the embrace of a thick, woollen blanket
on a frosty winter night
or the shimmying hips of a cool breeze
on a humid, standstill afternoon

and how can I possibly decide
what is more beautiful

the feel of the dove's feathers
against my fingers .

...or against my heart

the singsong patterns of the foam
across sleepless, moon-blazed oceans
or the lonely branches, of an almond tree
...casting shadows, across my sleepy face

moments that I try to preserve,
inside my fragile pages, like painted snowflakes
or the ones that I have yet to live

the wonder...
in a deliriously happy baby's eyes

or the hope..
..in a terminally ill person's soul

the softness that lives
within my mother's cheeks
or the strength that I feel
in her loving arms

tears, in someone's eyes...
for me
or in my eyes,
for them

but most of the times, it's the hardest to say
what I love more

you

or your memory.

I Breathe In

I breathe in...
The sights and smells
Of this city
I've come to know...
So well
I gaze...
Across the turquoise ocean
Where the waves
Liberate my spirit...
From its shell

I breathe in...
The brilliant sky line
Where the birds
Emerge shyly
From the dappled sunshine
I breathe in...
The gently...
Blowing winds
That soothe me
Like a mother, around her child

I breathe in...
The sounds of laughter
Pure and pretty
Like the golden-green butterfly
I'm always after
I breathe in...

The closeness,
I have always shared
With people,
Who almost knew me,
Almost cared

I breathe in...
The comfort
Of my home,
The safe walls,
The scents of childhood
On the pillows
I breathe in...the silence
Of my own heart
Aching with tenderness...
With memories..
Of home

I breathe... in...
The fragrance
Of love, and moist sand
The one...
His roses left...
On both my hands
And I just keep on breathing
Every moment
As much as I can
Preserving it, in my body
For the day
It can't

So I breathe in..
Once again..

Feeling life's energy
Fizzing through my cells
Never knowing
What awaits me
Or what's going to happen to me..
Next
I breathe in
This moment...
Knowing it's either life
Or it's death
I close my eyes,
And breathe in
Just believing in myself.

Sweet Tears

Slow down...oh sweet tears
...spilling down
My sad cheeks
Take it one drop...at a time
Come along...
Like silk breeze
Hang on...to my lashes
Paint your diamonds...
On their tips
Soak me up...
And all my secrets
Just be careful...not to slip

Slow down...oh sweet tears
You're burning down...a hot trail
You are falling, always falling
I have nothing...to replace
Hold on...just hold on...
Your value....is far too much
To be lost somewhere...in a puddle
Even you deserve...a fond touch

Slow down...oh sweet tears
You're always tearing me...apart
Crawl...crawl...into someone's hands
And all the way...into their heart
Slow down...oh sweet tears
Sometimes...you have to wait

But there's no rush at all...not yet
Someday...you will be wiped away

Slow down...and you will see
Your destination....was never far
From my lashes...to my cheeks
You're a blink away...from the stars
Slow down...oh sweet tears
...gushing river...down my face
Take it one drop at a time,
Like petals in the rain

Hang on...and you will find
All the things...that you have missed
Don't fade away...unseen
This time...there is so much I have wished
Slow down...oh sweet tears
Flowing nectar...down my lashes' tips
Someday...
Someone...will kiss you away
Even before......you can reach my lips.

Too Delicate

Too tiny ...are...
a butterfly's wings
to bear the weight,
of my admiring gaze
so tiny...almost,
like a single flake of light
under the crush,
of an ebony sky

too restless....are...
the sandy feet of the waves,
to watch the dance
of my becalmed heartbeats
too high...above me,
are the glittering birds
to understand the love,
of my flightless arms,

so delicate are...your ears, my dear,
too delicate, for the ferocity,
in my caring words,
so oblivious, are all
these familiar faces around me,
to notice the affection
that stain my cheeks

too feeble ...are...
the furs of a kitten

too feeble...for even...
the gentlest brush of my fingers
too innocent...are..
the fluttering eyes of a child
to understand
my blazing need....to protect

so fragile are....your shoulders, my dear,
to make sense...of the fierceness,
in my embrace,
so magical is...your soft, baby skin,
to feel... the warmth...
of my ordinary touch

too shallow...are the canyons
under the oceans
in front of the depth
of my innermost being
too eternal...is all the love that I feel
to be contained..
in my mere...mortal body parts

too brittle...are...
the petals of these flowers,
to endure the storm
of my tears,
and too delicate is ....your heart, my dear,
to bear the weight,
of my tenderness.

For My Mother

You will always be,
That first streak of light at dawn,
To pour its golden syrup, into the slumber of my eyes,

You will always be,
That first diamond, on each blade of grass
To sparkle like a newborn's first teardrop in the world,

The thoughts of you,
Will always be, that first gust of wind,
To blow away my tumbleweed of Monday's anxieties
That silver, rust-proof master-key
To release from my heart, the birds of yesterday

You will always be, that first raindrop
To quench,
Love's drought...from my soul,
That first scent, to waft in....through an open door

You will always be,
The first firefly I catch, in my nostalgia's jar,
Even as summer fades, and wrinkles

That most beautiful smile I see,
Even when I cut my 80th birthday cake

You will always be,
That first rush of warmth I feel

When I snuggle into my childhood's blanket
The only pillow....that I rest my tired, dreamy head on

The first note,
In my most heartfelt gratitude's symphony
That timeless star, that shoots across the sky,
Every time I blink

You will always be, my sweet mother,
That first meadow, to bloom on my praying lips

The most velvety curtain drawn,
Over storm windows to keep me safe,

Your gentle kiss,
That first brushstroke
To design the lines in my palms

And I want you to know, my dear Mum
That you always were,
And always will be...

That first ever touch, to have fertilized
The ground....beneath my life's trees

And that first ever rose, to have fragranced
The rest of my memories.

Fleeting Moments

Who am I....to try and stop,
The sun, from setting, the day...from dissolving,
Into the magma of time, when we're all...only just passing,
Like a fragrance in the wind...on this unexplained voyage
With our feet...grape-squashed in memories
Our skins still flushed...from the touch of summer's lips
For I can only allow the threads of time, to embroider your lovely
face,
Bracket the joy in your smile, and leave out the confusion
For it's up to you and me, to take solace...in nostalgia's arms
And our ability...to create the everlasting, from fleeting moments.

Romancing Poetry

So what
If you are not here, my dear,
This poetry, I will romance

Nuzzle myself
Against the warmth of these words
With my ice cold hands

Light up
This deep, dark tunnel of my soul
With the thoughts of you,
Through my flaming pen

Tangle my hair
Around these metaphors
Drenched, in the memory
Of your skin, your scent

My weary back, I shall rest
Against each pillow-soft line
Slowly exhale, my yearning heart,
All over the page

Comfort myself, with the thin fabric
Of every rhyme I've spun
And wait for you,
In this bed of verses, I've made

So what
If you are not here, my dear,
Within this poetry, I shall dance

Within these walls,
Bind my feet,
To one and only rhythm
In the dim light of your arms

And shut my eyes,
As the tears start to flow,
In ink, towards you,

All the while,
Pretending this poetry, is the home
You will someday come back to

And I shall write, my dear,
For as long as I can,
Write till the day,

To me, you return

And when you won't
When you tell me,
You do not ever want to

I'll set fire
To these words

And wait to burn.

Oh Poetic Minds

Oh! Poetic Minds!
Such wonders you are of mankind!
Each unique in your golden thoughts
So many lessons to the world you've taught!

Oh! Your Poetic Pens!
So much richer than successful men!
Each bubbling like a fountain of youth!
So reminiscent...of simple truths!

Oh! Your Poetic Eyes!
Such freedom they reflect in the skies!
Each as radiant as an exotic bird
So much deeper than a spoken word

Oh! Your Poetic Touch!
So much warmer...than one's own blood!
Each like a cradle in my lover's arms
Drops of eternity...on my very palms

Oh! Your Poetic Tears!
Such sadness you have poured through your fears!
But each rising like a fragrant haze
So tenderly you glide over the page

Oh! Your Poetic Hearts!
Such compassion you share in your art!
Each filled...with a love so deep
While you help rest of the universe sleep

Oh! ....Poetic Souls!
Such strength lies in your varied roles!
You may be a parent, a sister, or a child
But your pain and happiness is worthwhile!

Oh! Poetic Minds!
Such wonders you are of mankind!
Such beauty....such purity...I see in your words
Oh Poetic Minds!....You are taking over the world.

Sometimes The Rain

Sometimes,
the rain falls for the birds,
Softly...subtly,
In little baubles, of silver milk,
To cuddle clean, delicate feathers
To fall sleep...inside their wings

Sometimes, it falls
In rich abundance,
For farmers, waiting...
With parched hearts
& starving cattle,
Upon dream-sown fields

Sometimes,
it comes in easy, playful drops,
For children, eager to
Splash and squelch,
Their way home...from school

Sometimes it falls
In white hot thrashes,
And thunders
To fill the insatiable stomachs
Of restless seas

Sometimes,
It falls with the roughness,

Of a sisal,
To scrub the city pure,
Of its secrets, darkness, and dirt,
With moonlit beads

Sometimes,
The rain pours...just for the lovers
In gentle, shimmery flutters
A million drops, becoming one
As two lush lips...finally meet

Sometimes...like a wrist-full of bangles,
To simply dispel,
The silence,
Sorrows have weaved

Sometimes,
It falls.....to let go,
The murky clouds of its past,
And embrace its rosy future

To let its own wounds wash away,
Along with those, of others
....it has healed

Or sometimes,
It just falls,
For you and me
To be the violin, playing in the background
Of our loneliness's song

But....Above all,
the rain...the beautiful rain

Falls for itself
Hitting, the earth hard

Simply to salute...
The sheer joy

Of being
Alive.

I Thought

I thought...I was melting
Into the arms of the wind
My inner being... as light...
As a diamond dove's breath
I thought...I was falling
Like a nimble-footed rain
Dancing...to the melody
Of heaven's purity
And I felt my eyes...
Suddenly...turn aqueous
As if the muffled blue
Of the underwater
Had risen...to greet me
Spraying little, salty droplets
Of love's tenderness
Upon...my dreamy eyelids
I thought...I was breathing
In contentment's womb
In its all-encompassing warmth
So far away....
From my sorrow's tomb
My peeling skin,
Rinsed fresh, and anew
I thought, oh I thought
I was coming together,
Limb by limb, after being broken,
For an infinity
My spirit, in the hands of...

Affection's sculptor
...That I was unfolding,
Petal by petal,
Each reflecting the colour,
Of a healing bruise,
And my heart,
Lay ensconced...in such peace
That I wondered...
...If I was even...alive
I thought,...oh I thought,
The stars...
Had pressed my skin, with a kiss,
As soft and swirling....as a feather
And as, I floated...awake
I realized, finally,
I had been safe in bed, sleeping

Next to my mother.

The Gaze of Love

Nothing goes...

Disregarded

Under..
That tender gaze...
Of love

Not a single...
pearl of teardrop

Nor the
Slightest flutter...
...Of a dove

The ugly...
Become beautiful

The feeble...
Strong

Wounds become
...unborn stars

And the living

...Immortal...

An everlasting song.

I'll Always Remember

I'll always remember
The kindness in your words
That you whispered into my spirit
When I needed it the most

I'll always remember
The sparkle of pure joy
In the impoverished boy's eyes
When I offered him my food

....these damp, misty mornings
All my memories of the rain
Almost enchanting me, back to sleep

All the things my mother said
The feel of her soft cheeks
And the luxury, of breathing in her scent

...These ever singing wind chimes
Soothing my weary nerves
In their own magical language

I'll always remember...the laughter
Down these corridors
Of some long forgotten time
When so much simpler...was life
The sudden heat, shimmering
When he wrapped me, in his kiss

And turned me...almost liquid
I'll always remember..

The hand...that gave me sustenance
And the arms...that gave me shelter
I'll always remember

All the promises,
That I made,
And all my mistakes,

The look in the puppy's eyes,
When I stroked his soft furs

The sweet dimple..in my lover's chin
And the fire...beneath his skin

I'll always remember...

Those chilly nights in December
Bonfires, and smiling faces
And the light of God...in the embers
I'll always remember...

All the people
Who fluttered...
In an out...of my life

I'll always remember,
Deep in my heart

Even if I am the first...
To be forgotten.

Morning Arrives

Oh how....
Oh how I remember those times...
When morning used to arrive, wearing a frilly, cotton frock,
With her long, golden hair dusted in sea breeze
The skies diving, into the blue of her eyes,
She used to stand behind those curtains, smiling at me,

And I'd always wonder, is it possible?
For someone, to look so astonishingly beautiful,
To have their cheeks always kissed, by two fresh peonies,
To wear earrings, plucked straight from the poppy fields?

I'd always admire, the way she moved,
So gracefully between my bedroom and the sky,
The way she came wafting, from the kitchen,
With the aroma, of freshly baked breads, and blueberry pies

Oh how I'd bask in the enchanting, sun-warmed fragrance of her hair,
In her soft, motherly arms, as she carried me,
Through the day, and through the years,
As I watched her grow with me, from silly pinks, to elegant whites,
From pop tarts and potato chips, to strict, low-carb diets,

Sometimes, she came decorated,
in my night's dreams
Some other times, she sang melancholy tunes,
Knowing just what I'd need,
We'd always share, our deepest secrets

Writing letters to each other, upon the winds
And some other times, she'd draw me lazy rainbows
Just so she could see me smile

She always listened,
To my heavy, crestfallen sighs
Creeping into my lonely, lavender-printed quilt,
Until one day, I finally got to share her
With the love of my life...

Oh...how I remember her beauty, in every season,
In the greenest of springs, and palest of winters
In laughter and in freedom

But today...oh today,
There's something about her...
That looks...a little different..

As I watch her come knocking, upon my window
I mourn the loss, of her radiance
Her beautiful features hidden, in a black veil of despair
She no longer looks, the queen that she is,

As she calls out my name ....

But there's nothing I can do,
to comfort her, ...nothing,
so instead I lie here in my bed,
And watch her heart break
Today, she looks just like a widow to me,
For I....refuse to wake.

I Live There

I live there....
High atop the floating mountains,
Where the wind glitters through my hair,
I live there...

Where the sun can be spotted
Everywhere,

When it weeps,
A place where your feet can climb,
But never reach

Where sweet hyacinths bloom,
When they fall, my tears
Tears,
Which your hands can touch,
But never really feel

I live there...
Far above the song-filled clouds,
Where the dewdrops touch my skin so bare,
I live there...

Where the soft melodies flow,
Everywhere

When it sings,
A song your ears can listen,
But never touch your lips
Where cruel words, have no meaning
they make an empty sound

Cruel words,
which your heart can spill,
But never abound

I live there...
Farther beyond the misty skies,
Where every whisper is a sincere prayer
I live there...

Where the birds are infinite
Everywhere

Where they flee,
It's a place your eyes can wander,
But never see

Where everyone accepts me,
Without any pretence

It's a place your mind can picture,
but never really comprehend

I live there,
Where the moon lies down beside me ,
Where stars blanket me everywhere,
I live there...

Where the wind glitters through my hair,
Where I open my eyes,
and sweet faces light up everywhere
Where they love me
And care
I live there....

It's Always You

It's always you,
against a feathery blue sky,
with your lopsided rainbow smile,
and twinkly eyes,

it's always you,
behind the old barbed wire fence,
standing arm in arm,
with a wildly fruiting tree,

you,
in your barefooted romance
with the warm white sands,
wearing your favourite sports cap,
and monkey-printed shorts,

you,
squished between spring,
and summertime, with happiness trickling
like melted cheese down your chin

it's always you,
lying spread-eagled on the bed,
with flecks of sun caught breathless
upon your handsome cheekbones

you,
shaking the liquid kiss, of raindrops
off your over-quenched skin

it's always you, standing right there
in your chequered shirt,
with your hands tucked somehow,
in the pockets of my heart,

you
staring right into the eyes
of something only you can see,
the heat of your gaze,
somehow scorching me,

you,
puckering your song-kissed lips,
with a guitar on your lap,
tugging at my soul's strings,

it's always you,
beneath everything I know,
beyond everything I see,
you,
your presence,
burning in my life's hearth
but somehow frozen in time

it's always you, right there
and it's always me, right here,

lost in a photograph.

The Sound of Your name

The sound, of your name
So soft, so soothing
Like the tapping, of the rain
The sound, of your name

The sound, that each morning,
The birds, long to hear
The sound, that so naturally
Sweeps away, all my fears

When whispered,
What an exquisite
Song, it makes

On my lips,
Like the tingle, of sweet,
And sour grapes

The sound, of your name

Like a shawl,
Of sweet safety
Around,
My fragile body

The only echo,
In the mountains,
The forests, and valleys

The sound of your name
The candle, to my flame

The sound, that keeps my stars,
Burning, and bright
The sound, which is my pillow
Of comfort, each night

The sound, of your name

A great companion, to my loneliness,
The balm, to all my pains
The sound of your name

The lighthouse, in my dreams
The voice, of the sun's rays

The only thing of value
Of a life that's gone in vain

The sound of your name

The greatest of hopes,
Upon which I have ever lain

And the only melody,
That my heart has ever played.

The way you kill me

It's the way you kill me,
With sweet poison in your eyes
You pour it down my lips,
My warm, bleeding life
You drip down my veins,
Like tears, not cried,
And you only taste sweeter,
When I scream, and die

It's your name upon my tongue,
Like carvings on a tomb
Your scent is, everywhere,
Like black, toxic fumes
And it's how you kill me,
With no word, from you
As I turn almost instantly,
From blood red, to ice blue

It's your grip on my neck,
But for you I can breathe
Your fingers kiss my flesh,
Like death kiss the seas
And you kill me once again
Every time you ignore me,
When I lie down and wait
For you to come and bury me

It's your ashes in my heart,
Like dust on an old blade

But before I can rise,
I am consumed, in fresh flames
You kill me a million times
With a promise, of new pain
And you walk away this time,
Killing me, in cold shame

And it's how you kill me
With sweet poison in your eyes,
And as if that's not enough
You whip out another knife,
I scream, and I bleed,

And let out... the sweetest cry
Because the way you kill me,
Is just the way...I wanna die....

I Do Not Want To Miss a Single Thing

I do not want to miss, a single thing,
The summers, nor falls
Monsoon, nor springs
I do not want to miss, a single thing,
I want to taste the winters, of every place
Look at every naked tree, touch the snowflakes,
I want to kiss every flower, that blooms in the meadows
Watch every raindrop, patter against the window
I want to watch the grass sway, in every other field,
I want to rest in every hammock, between coconut trees
I do not want to miss, a single thing
I want to hear the exotic call, of every bird in the jungles,
Be amazed by the cracks of lightning, and hear each thunder's rumble,
Hold the sand of a thousand beaches, and feel it run through my fingers,
Drive my car through every tunnel, and drench myself in mountain rivers,
I do not want to miss, a single thing,
I do not want to blink,
For fear I might miss the birth of a smile on your face,
For fear that the pigeon, may flutter away,
I do not want to sleep,
For fear I might miss the twinkle of the brightest star,
For fear I may never know,
How the moon glimmers, in the darkest hour,
I do not want to miss, a single thing
I do not want to miss the meals my mother cooked
Or when I wore my favourite dress,

and the way he would have looked!
I do not want to miss, a single thing,
I want to hear my father chuckle,
each time over his favourite movie scene,
I want to hear every anecdote, of my brother in his teens
I do not want to miss, a single thing,
I want to hear every coo, of my baby in the future,
Kiss away each wound; watch every crinkle of laughter,
I do not want to miss, a single thing,
I want to be there, when each joke, each story is shared,
Over crackling fires, I want to feel each and everyone's care
I do not want to miss a single thing,
I want to breathe in each scent that sparkles in the air,
I want to be here, and at the same time, be everywhere
I want to read every book that's written,
Hear every song that was sung,
I want to gaze at every cloud,
And hold the zing of each fruit, on my tongue
I do not want to miss, a single thing
From everything that is, and ever will be,
Between my first and last spring,
I do not want to miss....a single thing

Lover's Night

Let your eyes do the smiling
Envelop me in velvet fire
Let your lips do the beguiling
Oh make me tremble with desire!

Let your hands do the whispering,
The lullabies, of honeyed hunger
Let your voice, do the whimpering
Sparkle me in crashing thunder!

Let your hair, do the teasing
Play my fantasies soft and wild
Let your skin, do the pleasing
Make my womanhood come alive!

Let your body do the sweltering,
Burn in me like crimson wine
Let your arms do the sheltering,
Oh wrap me 'round this lover's night!

Let your scent do the lingering,
Sink deep into my folds
Let your warmth do the comforting
Just flow into my soul

Let your charm do the swirling
Make me glitter in star gold
Let your love do the twirling,
Oh let's watch this night unfold!

Let the stars, do their dreaming,
As they watch us from above
Let the skies do their speaking
Of how we made, beautiful love

And let our memory, do the breathing,
The night is still lush
And this time,
Let my heart do the beating
For the both.of us.

Great Things

As the sky prepares to settle its tired, aching feet
Into the night's velvet slippers

I settle, into my armchair, soaking the teabag,
Of my thoughts, into warm liquid-y stars

Pondering, opportunities, that sailed away from me
Like childhood paper boats

Wondering, about my grand plans...
That somehow dissolved...into oblivion

Counting all the pages, that I failed to turn
And the steps, that I never took

Trying to remember,
All the great things I've done,

But the truth is, I haven't, really

I've never...
Broken a record, in my entire life,
Or won an award
Never gotten close to writing
A totally flabbergasting, beautiful poem

Never scored above an 80 percent,
In any test or exam
Or made it onto the front page, of the local newspaper

Never got around to being an idol,
To my younger siblings
Or the perfect daughter to my parents

I never bagged...my dream job
Or worked hard enough...to build my nest
Upon the treetops of success

Never followed the path....that I should have

Or dreamed....with eagle wings

Never rescued a tree,
From being cut down

Or really saved...Anybody's life...

I've done no such things that I can boast of

And yet,
Sitting here in my armchair,
I smile...to myself, under a moon
Glinting down at me, sequined in silver pride

All because,
Someone smiled today,
And always will,

Because of me.

When I Write...

When I write
It feels like I am home...
After a million centuries, of drifting at sea,
Among the glitter, of familiar faces I am
A stranger to myself, no more

When I write...
I am in the fond arms, of a childhood friend,
Upon whose colourful heart, I can hang
The charcoal drawings, of my woes

I am like water...coming to boil
Evaporating, in silver fumes
When I write of dusk and doom

I am a pirouetting dancer...
Dancing...
In a celestial auditorium
The audience...being my own reflection

When I write...
I am that crushed bud blossoming...
The one that the bees and butterflies...
Gave up on...a long time ago

I am that dust, forever swirling
In any direction,
That the wind blows

I am a cheap digital camera
Trying to capture every moment
So that time slows

When I write...
I am simply...a calm brook
Flowing peacefully
Wherever my pen takes me

I am under God's wings
That keep me sheltered
By whispering words to me

When I write,
I am everything
That I want to be
Everywhere..
That I want to be

I am that little grin
On a child's summer kissed face
A unique mixture
Of every emotion, that can be traced

And when I write...
I am simply,
A dead soul awakening

Coz when I write
I am finally
I am finally...breathing.

My Favourite

It's only you who can do this to me...my love,
Only you, who can make sepia
Seem, like my favourite colour, to eyes...accustomed
To a more kaleidoscopic world,
it's only you, who can make autumn mist,
taste like champagne and winter rain taste
like the elixir of life itself
Who can make the smell of old diaries,
Wrinkled words, my favourite fragrance,
Who can make...the dusky, falling sky of solitude,
Seem like my favourite hour of the day
It's only you....my love, this can only be ...your handiwork,
Who can turn the murmurs of melancholia,
Into a paradise-bird's song
Who can make reminiscence as comforting
as hot, sandalwood bath soaks,
It's only you.... because of you,
That I savour slow ballads...like exotic herbs on my tongue
That I bite into sad, classic poems, as if they were a cupcake,
Only you can make it seem...like my favourite thing to do,
Who can make loneliness, my favourite tree to sit under,
And shadows, like a soft, springy mattress to rest upon
It's only you...who can make anticipation
Seem like my favourite ride, imagination...my favourite exercise,
Who can fill dreaming, with more oxygen than breathing,
It's only you,
who can knife me...with the honey of memories
make emptiness....seem like my favourite corner of myself,

who can haunt me, with far away embraces,
and it's only you, my love, only you
who can make...this sweet pain of longing
seem like...my favourite feeling.

Speeding Train

Like a speeding train
I am passing by...
I don't know
Where I'm heading
With whom, or why
All I know is that....
I will never, ever,
Pass from here again
All I know is I'm skidding forward
On this track of life

And I know I'm always moving
From station to station
No place resembles home
I have no destination
All strangers journey with me
No one bothers,
With my name
But no matter, their countless number
There's always,
An empty space

Their scents waft through me
Some familiar, some faint
Words they whispered,
Dreams they shared,
Are all the memories, that I made
But how long ?

Till I have the luxury,
To see,
The same face
And once I have passed,
I know, nobody will wait for me,
At the same place

And I pass through the valleys,
Through the deserts, and rain
Sometimes it feels like
I'm the only one who's moving
While the rest of the world remains
And I'm moving so fast
I'm missing out,
on every sight, and every grain
Through the murky tunnels,
And gaping emptiness,
I am just chasing myself again

I am nothing but a speeding train
Speeding through life
Steering alone the forked paths,
With no one, by my side

I am nothing but an echo...
There's just smoke I leave behind
And when I look to the sky,
I see myself ....as I am
A blur in the human mind.

My Beauty

I keep my kindness in my eyes
Gently folded around my iris
Like a velvety, brown blanket
That warms my vision

I keep my shyness in my hair
Tucked away into a ponytail
Looking for a chance to escape
On a few loose strands in the air

I keep my anger on my lips
Just waiting to unleash into the world
But trust me; it's never in my heart
It evaporates into words

I keep my dignity upon my chin
Like a torch held up high
For those who have betrayed me
Radiating a silent, strong message

I keep my gratitude in my smile,
A glistening waterfall in the sun
Gently splashing at that person,
Who made me happy for some reason

I keep my sensitivity in my hands
Reaching out for your wet cheek
Holding you, with all the love
The love I want to share, and feel

I keep my passion in my writing
My words breathing like fire
Screeching against an endless road
As I continue to be inspired

I keep my simplicity in my soul
Spread over me like a clear sky
Reflecting all that I am
And all that's ever passed me by

And I hope you will look
Beyond my ordinary face,
My simple, tied hair,
My ordinary tastes
And I hope you will see me,
From everyone...apart
As I keep my beauty...in my heart.

Tomorrow Came

Tomorrow came,
with a squirt of sunshine,
and some dew, ordinarily...almost
with its trademark, freshly whipped skies,
night-cleansed breeze,
with its paintbrush always dipped
in the season's colours

tomorrow came,
like a hand-arranged bouquet,
from a secret admirer,
with a gentle knock & agile footsteps,
with the splash of many surprises,
with the tanginess...of all things new,

it came clothed in promises,
& bejewelled in hope, drenched...
In the scent of sanguinity,
with the glow of revelations,
moments playing...the flute of opportunities,
of new beginnings, bringing along
...a buzzing, under my fingernails,

sometimes it came with much fanfare,
sometimes, with mute tears,
waiting in the distance....like old folks

but tomorrow came...like it always does,
with the briefness of a sigh,
with the silky, slippery tiptoe of rain
with the temporary warmth...of held hands

like a charming bird upon the porch
that I know...will soon fly away

it came bursting...out of time's cocoon...
melting...into everything...
that once belonged to today,

...with the superficial magic
of summer romances,

Tomorrow came,
With the illusion of today,
Even more fleeting than yesterday,

It came,
like it always comes,
And went...like it's always gone,
like a favourite song in its final seconds
Tomorrow came, and left
Leaving nothing...
Nothing...
but a familiar....
lingering...sense of loss behind.

My Muse

What is it...about you?
That tugs at me...deep inside
That gets me skittering...in the wind
That's delicious...to my poetic side
What is it...that you do?
To make my whole world...come alive
Tell me..how do you stand there?
Filling the doorway....of my life

There you are
And there's....
That intensity...in your eyes
Soft and swirling, just enough
To burn my pen...as I write
There you are
And there's...
That glimmer...of your smile
Shy and blossoming, just enough
To flood the canvas...of my mind

What is it...that you do?
To make me feel...these intense feelings
To wrench my heart...round a blank paper
That has my world reeling
What is it...about you?
That seems to sweeten...my deepest longings
That makes me believe...I can flutter high
And fill this emptiness...by simply writing

There you are
And there's...
That delicate sculpt...of your lips
Soft and pink, but just enough
To make me feel...kissed
You really...must be something
To have moved me...like this
But how....will I truly depict you?
You're perfect, my writing isn't

And there you are
And there's...
That black silk...of your hair
Casting a spell when the wind blows
All I can do is stare!
There you are
And there's...
That warm sun...of your care
And all I have...is just one wish
To be standing right there

But in the end,
I know
I know I will be nothing to you
No matter who I am,
And no matter what I do,
In the end, I know
You aren't mine....to choose
So if not anything,
Will you please....remain my muse?

The World is thinning

The world is thinning
Even though the earth is spinning

One by one it seems to me
They're all leaving

Like oceans receding
When I'm not dreaming

Broken shells piercing...
My soul...it's bleeding

The world is thinning
Though my eyes are searching...

For an old comforting place
The sun feels watery on my face

Memories are waning
Trickling down, I'm shaking

Where I once stood here believing
Today... I'm kneeling

The world is thinning
Though my hands are reaching

For that same, slippery grasp
That same hourglass sand

The crowd is fading
All the promises are breaking

In thick air I was breathing
In complete loneliness I'm freezing

The world is thinning
Don't know if I'm losing or winning

The sky above is shifting
Fallen leaves are drifting

The birds are no more flying
The rain is no more crying

One by one, it seems to me
They are all dying...

The world is thinning
And the earth...it's still spinning

My world is thinning
And it's all because of one person I'm missing.

My Love

My love is a velvet couch
Gently easing you,
At the end of a tiring day
My love is a shimmering cloud,
Watching over you,
Like an angel all night and day
My love is a thoughtful whisper,
Always assuring you
Like a best friend in the dark
My love is a small picture,
That can fit anywhere
In the frame of your heart

But my love is too soft
To ever, be heard
My love is too heavy
To be contained, in words
My love is too deep
For you, to understand
My love is too steep
To be held, in your hands

But my love, is a winter's mist,
Gently dissolving, through the window
At the nape of your neck
My love is a moth's wings,
Fluttering around the warm candle,
To see if you peacefully slept
My love is a lost treasure,
To which you are alone

The one and only key
My love is a white feather
Swirling across your skin
Pure and free

My love is hard to explain
But easy to feel
My love is steeped in pain
But ready to heal
My love is far too ordinary
For you to see
And in the end,
My love is nothing
But an incomplete story

But my love, is a powerful weapon
A bullet which pierces,
The very heart and soul
My love is an unbreakable bond
A lifelong promise
An endless spring of hope
My love is a starless night, a hidden moon
alive somewhere in the shadows
And my love, is the brightest smile
A hidden tear....waiting, to find its way home

My love is lonesome
But forever it will burn
My love is illiterate
But for you it shall learn
And my love will be there...
Wherever you turn
But my love is far too much
For you to return.

These little Expectations

When I sleep,
I just want to dream a little
When I wake up,
I just want to make it real
When I smile,
I just want someone to know it's for 'em
When I cry,
I just wish to be comforted by a friend
When I stay,
I just want to make it worthwhile
When I walk away,
I just want someone to follow me miles
When I speak,
I just want someone to understand my words
When I scream,
I just want someone to recognize my worth
When I care,
I expect a little in return
When I love,
I just hope that I cnn be the lucky one
And when I live,
I just want to make sure it's complete
When I die,
I just hope that I will be missed

You are this poetry

Do you know where you are?
You are in this poetry
I never thought you'd come
But I found you here, in front of me

Do you know you are the meaning?
Of these very words I write
And, without you, this poetry wouldn't make sense
Even if I wrote it in rhymes

Do you know it's you?
Who has filled up the spaces, between these alphabets!
And if you were like, really here with me
There would be no gaps at all, it'd be so perfect

Do you know it's you?
Who has breathed life into this phrasing!
Without you, these words would look so dead
Like they have no heart, no feelings

Do you know it's the colour of your eyes?
Those paint the background in royal shades?
And without you, no one would even read this
And all my efforts would be such a waste

Do you know it's your gentle smile?
That make these words flow honey smooth?
And without you, there would be jagged edges
And I would end up being the fool

Do you know it's your tender touch?
That make these words feel silky, soft?
And without you, I'd write so rough
And this poem would read just like thorns

Do you know it's your thoughts in my heart?
Those fill these words with so much warmth
And without you, these words would cry very much
And I would miss you, really a lot

Do you know it's all of you?
Who adds a bittersweet flavour to my poetry!
And without you, there'd be no taste
My life would have no story

Do you know it's all of you?
Who makes these words sing and dance?
And, without you, I'd never write
I wouldn't give my feelings a chance

Do you know it's my love for you?
That has brought you here , in this write
And without you, this poetry will have to end
With no farewells, and no goodbyes.

I Know

I know
I know what loneliness is
I have stared at it for hours...
Drowned myself in its cold shadow
And have never...emerged the same again...

I know
I know what beauty is
It's the sun rays sparkling on my fingertips
It's the green-blue bird ruffling its feathers
It's the way your eyes soften when you look at me

I know
I know what silence is
I have heard it echo off the walls of my house
Felt it burn my heart, burden my footsteps
And I've seen its sword hang between us

I know
I know what hunger is
I have seen it blaze in the eyes of the Poor
Seen it in the cracks and folds of their skin
I have fasted for My God and my flesh has felt it

I know
I know what happiness is
I've held it in my hands for fleeting seconds
I've felt it in the passing winds that toy with my hair
And even when it's gone I know it will come back again

I know
I know what jealousy is
It will stain the mirror for as long as I live
I have felt it settle comfortably in my bones
And that's why I know I will never be perfect

I know
I know what betrayal is
I have felt its icy slap on my heart
Heard what they talk about me behind my back
I know what it is to fall, fall down hard

And I know
I know what love is
I have seen its wonders beneath my eyelids
Pressed it deep against my chest so warm
Smiled a smile that still lingers on my lips

And I know
I know what hope is
I have seen it in all its glory
Felt it crumble through my hands, and found it again
Just exactly where I thought I had lost it.

Allow Me

Allow me, my dear
To bathe in the innocence of this moment,
In its marmalade-soft enchantment, with my hair
tangoing in the breeze, bronzed from the sun,
Scented, with the melody of songbirds,
As I lay curled and comforted, in the feathery lap of this morning
With postcard-pretty sights, caressing my eyes,
Flowers blushing and hushing, under my adoring gaze,
Let me...dance in this stillness, & sing in this silence,
With my feet snugly pressed, into the earth's sandals,
And allow the clouds...to come...fill my cup with love's tenderness
So I may share it with my dear ones,
To make them finally taste, the fragile words in my heart,
Oh let my cup be stained, with my mother's magenta lipstick,
and let its handles stay warm...from my father's touch,
The liquid inside, sugared, from my lover's reflection
For my cup is bottomless enough, to accommodate,
The depth...of my lyrical affection, so let me be
A butterfly once again, dusting my sparkly colors,
Like cinnamon flavorings, let me pour
Away this divine fluid into their hearts,
Down until the last drop, so the last sip may taste like
The first teardrop....
of an eternally flowing river.

In That Moment

I see you standing there
And my world stops for a moment
It's just you, your presence
Filling that moment
I feel my head float
My heart flips and rolls
It's just you, your warmth
And the sun above so golden
You smile your breathtaking smile
And the whole universe explodes in that moment
It's just you, your happiness
Colouring that moment
I feel a tingle on my skin
My cheeks twinkle into a hot pink
It's just you, you're radiance
And the sky above so brilliant
You walk towards me,
And all that matters is that moment
It's just you, everything about you
Completing that moment
The world is at our feet
It's a celebration of you and me
And all I need to live is in that moment...

I Cried with the night

I cried with the night
With the nightingales, and moonlight
With the dark, churning oceans
With the city, burnt in lights

Drip by drip, through my eyes
The stars grew dim, my tears bright
Like a beaded necklace, round my neck,
My chest grew warm, my bed moist

I cried, for every reason
For the millions stabs, in my back
For the breeze, no longer comforting
For my lone footsteps, in the sand

For familiar faces, turning cold
My tears new, but sorrows old
For my blanket, no longer soft
For the words I write, with no hope

I cried, till I couldn't breathe
Couldn't hold back, couldn't reach
Till my pain, swept over the world
Till my tears, swallowed all traces of me

One by one, washed clean
The sky grew bitter, my tears sweet
Like the taste of betrayal, upon my lips
The night grew darkest, my heart weak

And I cried, with the night
With lost friendships, love and lies
With the loss of my own desire, for living
With the heavens above, fading in lights

Drip by drip, through my eyes
My tears grew colorless, the hour bright
And I cried along,
With the passing night
Until it left me to rot,
In the morning light.

My moment of Sorrow

Sometimes, all I really need...is to be left alone
In my moment of sorrow, away...from the rest of the world,
Shaded by the oaks, nourished by the moon ,
without the burden of todays...or tomorrows,
judgments, or criticisms, under my galaxy,
of wounded stars, reading aloud...the fluent poetry
of my tears, until the storm in me...begins to subside,
And the strong currents...begin to calm, until I am nothing
but...a devastated shore, finally beginning to understand
What it means......to embrace myself.

I'd Trade

I'd trade
the emeralds fields
of June

and the white cashmere...
of December

life in the villas...chateaus,
and tomorrow's dancing slippers,

I'd trade
wishes...fulfilled
and warmth
tears...evaporated
... and tunes

and all just...
for a glimpse of you

Celebrate Life

Who needs an occasion?
To celebrate life
Each moment's a celebration,
Each morning, each night

Just to wake up to the sun
Is like being drunk on light
As if sipping with my skin
Its warmth and delight

To kiss my mother's hands
Is a celebration of tenderness!
Recalling times with my family
Like the fireworks of happiness

Just to watch the birds fly
Feels like sweet freedom
Where beauty meets melody
In each shade and each season

To play with little children
Is a celebration of innocence!
With the wind on my cheeks
Smiling in reminiscence

To stand up for somebody
Is a celebration of true friendship!
Just to know there'll always be
Someone who will fight it

To stroll down the beach
Is like being high on serenity
Along with sea turtles and baby crabs
Displaying divine creativity

To snuggle under the covers
Is a celebration of comfort!
Under a night laced with diamonds
Hugging my warm shirt

To sleep beside your beloved
Exhausted and content
Isn't the feeling of safety & completion?
A festivity of life itself

To whisper a small prayer
Is a celebration of faith!
Wishing, believing, and just living
In the hope of a better day

Just to be able to feel pain
Is like honoring this very existence!
Without these dark feelings
Would life still have magnificence?

We don't need an occasion
To celebrate and rejoice
Life itself is a celebration
Of love, and clouds, of simply being alive

And while loads of celebrations wait for us,
Let's begin, first, by raising a toast
To the stars, that never fail to shine,
And to the smiling faces,
Of the ones we love the most.

White Dove

My Sweet little dove,
Up above me you fly
Your gleaming white feathers
Like sunlit diamonds in the sky

How beautiful you are!
It makes me want to cry
As if an angel has descended
And gently kissed my eye

Everything I'll Leave Behind

Out of all the things I'll leave behind,
I will miss the feel of these warm summer nights
It's sweet embrace under the black satin sky
The tickle of whispers and his hand in mine

Out of all the things I'll leave behind
I will miss the wonder of a baby's smile
The sound of laughter and mischief of a child
The union of family and the gentleness in my mother's eyes

Out of all the things I'll leave behind,
I will miss the tiny celebrations of life
Cuddling in a blanket when it's cold outside
Steaming cups of coffee and fluffiness of the tide

Out of all the things I'll leave behind
I will miss the silence of the tears I cried,
For everything I had, for everything I couldn't
For everything I did, for everything I didn't
For everything I was, for everything I wasn't

For everything that lived, and everything that died
And for everyone I loved....more than my life.